God Knows Me!

from
❧ PSALM 139 ❧

by Joel Anderson
illustrated by Kristi Carter & Joel Anderson

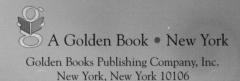

A Golden Book • New York

Golden Books Publishing Company, Inc.
New York, New York 10106

Dedicated to Cameron Lowe, age 8,
and his family, Michael, Lynda, Austin & Samuel Lowe

*All the days ordained for me were written in your book
before one of them came to be. Psalm 139:16*

"How do we keep our composure with the constant awareness
that Cameron's leukemia is uncertain? We know that God has
a plan for his life, whether it be 8 years or 98 years. Our
prayer is that his destiny be fulfilled and that he touch every
life that he is intended to touch."

O Lord, You see me
  and You know me.
You know when I sit down
  and when I stand up.
You even know
  what I am thinking!

Before I say a word,
You already know it.

You know when I go outside ...

or when I'm laying in my bed;
You know everything about me.

You protect me from all sides;
	You have placed Your hands around me.
Just thinking about this is so wonderful –
	it's too much for me to understand!

Where could I hide from You?

Could I ever run away from You?

If I went up in outer space, You are there.

If I went to the bottom of the ocean,
   You are there, too.

If I could fly past the clouds
   to the other side of the sea,
Your hand would hold me safely.

If I say, "Surely I can hide in the dark," even the darkness would be as bright as daytime to You.

You made every part of me.
You put me together while I was
    inside my mommy's tummy.
I praise You because I am wonderfully
    made. Your work is perfect.
Before I was even born, You saw me!
All of the days You have planned
    for me were written in Your
    book long ago.

Your thoughts are so important to me.
How many of them there must be!
If I tried to count them, they would be more than
all of the tiny grains of sand by the sea.

When I wake up in the morning,
I'm still with You.

Look at me, God. Look inside my heart.
See if I am sad or worried about anything.
See if I have done any bad things.
Show me how to love You
    forever and ever.